Primary Professional Development

The Deputy Headteacher's Handbook

Gill and Steve Jorgensen

Folens Publishers

Acknowledgements

Peter and Lucinda Neall

Ken Bevan

Folens allows photocopying of pages marked 'copiable page' for educational use, providing that this use is within the confines of the purchasing institution. Copiable pages should not be declared in any return in respect of any photocopying licence.

Editor: Alison MacTier   Layout artist: Barry Monks

Illustrations: Eric Jones   Cover image: 'Erasmus' by Hans Holbein the Younger

© 1999 Folens Limited, on behalf of the authors. Every effort has been made to contact copyright holders of material used in this book. If any have been overlooked, we will be pleased to make any necessary arrangements.

British Library Cataloguing in Publication Data. A catalogue record for this book is available from the British Library.

First published 1999 by Folens Limited, Dunstable and Dublin.

Reprinted 1999.

Folens Limited, Albert House, Apex Business Centre, Boscombe Road, Dunstable, LU5 4RL, England.

ISBN 1 86202 539-8

Printed in Singapore by Craft Print.

Contents

The schedules can be photocopied and used only within the confines of the purchasing institution.

The Deputy Head as manager

The role of Deputy Headteachers

The duties of a Deputy Headteacher were revised from 1 September 1994 to give them a clearer management perspective. A Deputy Headteacher has the same professional duties as a classroom teacher. In addition, a Deputy Headteacher is required to play a major role, under the direction of the Headteacher, in formulating the aims and objectives of the school, undertaking major responsibilities arising from the Headteacher's professional duties which have been reasonably delegated to him or her, and undertaking as necessary the full range of professional duties of the Headteacher in the event of the latter's absence from school.

A glance through the pay and conditions document illustrates the intention of the DfEE to define clearly every aspect of professional responsibilities. We are all aware of how clearly defined the school day, the curriculum and assessment have become. But even the 'powers-that-be' resort to vagaries when attempting a definition of the role of the Deputy Headteacher. This role is unique and your function will vary from school to school. However, from full-time class teaching deputies to those without class responsibility, there are principles which define your job and these do not vary.

As rapid change continues to be a characteristic of schools, the role of the Deputy is certainly altering within each establishment. This results in a job which has become much more significant and challenging.

A new statement of duties.

Management in schools

It is necessary to take one line of questioning from the introduction and resolve this issue. Is your primary function one of:

- ✔ assistant Headteacher
- ✔ leading teacher
- ✔ teacher representative?

Whether you are employed in a very small or an extremely large school, and whether or not you have class responsibility, recent legislation, recommendations in the Review Body Reports and the changing management emphasis have solved the dilemma.

If you have a full teaching timetable you will be better able to empathise with your teaching colleagues. Without a full teaching commitment you will have a greater overview of the organisation. Both roles enable you to bring extra qualities to support the overall management of the school.

The nature of management

✔ Management is the practice of bringing about results with and through other people.

✔ You have become a manager because you wish to have a greater positive effect than you can achieve by working alone.

✔ It is essential to understand that management is not an issue of power and control.

✔ A manager needs two important skills: those of organisation and, particularly, the ability to develop positive relationships.

✔ People want to be managed by managers who will help them to achieve their personal objectives.

A Deputy Headteacher must recognise that the best way to achieve objectives is to enable and support colleagues to succeed rather than taking on the full workload personally. This is a point that is often not appreciated by managers who subsequently become stressed and feel overwhelmed.

Managing colleagues

Delegating a task to a colleague who is not sufficiently skilled to do it is pointless and doomed to failure. Everybody wishes to succeed. Remember, however, that all are at varying stages of expertise.

Different strokes for different folks

It seems odd doesn't it? This means that consistency can be detrimental. Different people will require different forms of support. For example, an experienced member of staff may resent being told how to dot the i's and cross the t's. An inexperienced colleague may feel insecure if given a task but little assistance.

Supporting colleagues

There are four methods of support:

✔ assist – working together with a colleague

✔ advise – giving your opinion

✔ consult – discussing the issues

✔ delegate – leaving it to the other members of staff.

Leaving it to the other members of staff.

Effective management

Faced with a management issue, the prime consideration is always **the end result**. All choices and planning should occur with the end result in mind. It is tempting to concentrate on the 'way', in other words the process itself, and lose sight of what you are intending to achieve.

Be sure – if you keep hitting blockages you have chosen the wrong route!

This is a common feature in our schools, and is equivalent to a driver knowing that the M1 motorway is blocked at junction 10 yet continuing on the road and then complaining when they are jammed in a twenty-mile tailback.

If you are to be effective and manage supportively you must be clear about your position within the structure of the school. Many managers regard themselves near to or at the top of a hierarchical system. For some aspects this is acceptable but when viewing the Deputy Headteacher's role of support it is preferable to consider inverting the hierarchical triangle.

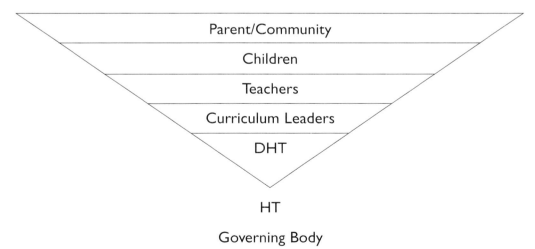

Empowering others

This is a directional model and its direction is defined by the long-term developmental plan of the school. The method of achieving objectives is one of enabling or empowering others to do their job well. It is the teacher's job to enable children to learn, the curriculum leader's job to enable colleagues effectively to teach each subject and the Deputy Headteacher's job to enable much of this to happen. In this model, the Headteacher/Governing Body lead on policy and the Deputy Headteacher assists with its implementation as well as its formation.

2

What are you managing?

There can be no definitive list of the Deputy Headteacher's responsibilities.

The Deputy Headteacher's responsibilities will depend upon:

✔ the size of the establishment
✔ the ethos of the school
✔ the expertise of your colleagues
✔ your teaching commitment
✔ your own experience and aptitudes.

Finally, and most importantly:

✔ the requirements of your Headteacher.
   In fact, it is not unusual when pursuing job advertisements to see requests for Deputy Headteachers to be in charge of the budget and the National Curriculum (that's clear enough!).

Job specification

The DfEE, in replying to recommendations, states that good practice occurs when 'the Deputy is in partnership and participation with the Headteacher rather than simply giving assistance.'

When applying for the post of Deputy Headteacher you will have your own ideas and expectations.

When applying for the post of Deputy Headteacher you will have your own ideas and expectations; these however, may differ from those of your Headteacher. Without clarification this can result in a poor working relationship and lack of job satisfaction.

It is advisable that existing Deputies or those newly appointed ask their Headteacher to set a date, approximately one term in advance, when a full discussion leading to a negotiated job specification can occur. Use this first term to observe, to discuss with colleagues and to formulate your own audit of your role within the school.

A weekly sheet that can be used to record observations and duties undertaken will be useful in providing a summary for your discussion (see Schedule 1). This summary should not be emotive or judgmental.

Major duties undertaken

Curriculum

Internal organisation

Staff development

Outside agencies

Pastoral

Administration

Observations (aspects which need review or development)

1.

2.

3.

4.

Week ending _____

This sheet should be completed quickly in order to record impressions which will be helpful when negotiating your job description. These sheets are for your own use only and need to be summarised.

Negotiating your job specification

It is essential that uninterrupted time is set aside for this task. It may be necessary to hold the meetings out of school hours but the mutual benefits of such meetings to both Headteacher and Deputy Headteacher will prove to be time well invested. Before you start to negotiate a job specification there is an important concept which needs to be fully grasped.

Negotiations need not mean compromise

It is often advised when negotiating to accept a compromise. A compromise can be ineffective and negative; it essentially means fifty per cent loss as well as fifty per cent gain. This loss can and often does result in feelings of frustration and can be a prime demotivator. There is a distinction between compromise and negotiation. Dictionary definitions illustrate the difference:

Compromise – a settlement of dispute by mutual concession.
Negotiate – confer with others to reach an agreement.

Keep this definition in mind when negotiating your job specification, then every issue can be viewed by concentrating on objectives.

Perhaps at this juncture it is necessary to address the possibility of disagreement. If the Headteacher states that he or she wishes you to undertake a particular responsibility such as an area which you consider will not assist in achieving overall objectives or one in which you have little interest:

What do you do?

You have a choice/consequence situation:

Choice	Positive consequence	Negative consequence
1. Agreeing to take the responsibility	Avoiding conflict	Undertaking a job which you don't want
2. Token agreement	Avoiding conflict	Differing expectation, poor communication
3. Stating your concerns and accepting the job	Clear communication, showing support for the management structure, non-confrontational, honesty	Still doing the job
4. Saying no	Not doing the job	Conflict, resentment, undermining the Headteacher, poor teamwork

Having considered the positive and negative consequences of available choices, you are better able to consider which will best suit your overall objective.

Choice/consequence

Difficulty —

— —

— —

Choice	Positive consequence	Negative consequence

Choose the consequence which is most in line with what you want.

The job specification

It is sensible for a job specification to be negotiated and regularly reviewed. This gives a golden opportunity to produce a clear and concise working document. It must never be allowed to become a token exercise whereby the job specification resides in the filing cabinet until its next review.

Section 1 of the job specification

The first section will outline general areas of responsibility. It should allow for contingencies such as the absence of the Headteacher and even the long-term absence of a curriculum leader. The popular, favourite blanket statement 'and any other request made by the Headteacher' should be avoided.

If a situation arises whereby the Headteacher wishes the Deputy to take major additional responsibilities, this should be a matter for renegotiation, for example, in the event of a non-class teaching Deputy having to cover for a long-term absence there would have to be a change in some areas of agreed responsibility.

. . . and any other request made by the Headteacher.

Section 2 of the job specification

The second section will translate the general responsibilities into a working and planning format containing both short- and long-term objectives. These objectives should be given time boundaries and agreed upon as being realistic and achievable.

Section 3 of the job specification

This section should outline any support that you will require in order to achieve these objectives. This support may take the form of advice, resources and/or in-service training.

Finally, this is an opportunity for the Deputy to consider his or her career and seek assistance in its development, for example, a class teaching Deputy may have little working knowledge of budget management and could require provision to familiarise him- or herself with the systems.

We would suggest that the job specifications be available to all members of staff. In fact, all the short- and long-term objectives of every 'job specification' should relate to the overall school developmental plan. Examples of sample generic job specifications are included as Schedules 3 and 4. The duties outlined in these examples will provide ideas. We envisage that sections 1, 2 and 3 are negotiated because of individual circumstances.

Sample job specification for Deputy Headship

The Deputy Headteacher will be expected to:

1. ensure that school policy is carried out effectively

2. support the Headteacher in promoting the aims and objectives of the school and ensure that all staff are aware of any changes that may be made

3. assume the responsibilities of the Headteacher during his or her absences from school

4. help and advise other members of staff, particularly NQTs, student teachers and those newly appointed to the school

5. advise on and assist with the implementation of a discipline policy throughout the school

6. be involved with group discussion on curriculum planning

7. share overall responsibility with the Headteacher for all aspects of the curriculum

8. be responsible together with the Headteacher and class teachers for the pastoral care of all children

9. share responsibility with the Headteacher for the collection, disbursement and bookkeeping of the school fund

10. share responsibility with the Headteacher for the school budgeting

11. be responsible for keeping and circulating the minutes of staff meetings

12. be responsible for a rota of staff duties, including assemblies; substituting replacements when necessary

13. share responsibility with the Headteacher for admission procedures

14. be responsible for deployment of staff on a day-to-day basis

15. coordinate timetabling in conjunction with curriculum leaders and class teachers

16. facilitate the release of post holders (when possible) to carry out their duties in relation to their area of the school curriculum

17. take over the responsibility for curriculum areas when there are vacancies in the school establishment

18. collect from the staff, and present to the Headteacher, a copy of their planned class programmes at the beginning of each half-term

19. take on the role of class teacher either as cover, or as part-time or full-time support as the school situation dictates.

Sample job specification for Deputy Headship

The Deputy Headteacher will be expected to:

1. assume the responsibility of the Headteacher in his or her absence from the premises

2. be in charge of the bookkeeping for the school fund

3. organise the collection and disbursement of such funds under the direction of the Headteacher

4. be responsible for the organisation of such rotas as may be needed for the efficient running of the school and will make such substitutions as are necessary, including substitutions for staff absent from class teaching situations

5. coordinate staff requisitions and supervise the presentation of these to the Headteacher

6. order books and equipment for children and staff as directed by the Headteacher

7. advise on and assist with all discipline matters

8. be entitled to refer any matter to the Headteacher

9. be responsible for the checking of all items on the stock book and to inform the Headteacher of any necessary repairs or replacements

10. be responsible for keeping minutes of all staff meetings and to represent the Headteacher in any group discussion about curriculum matters if the Headteacher is not present

11. coordinate, advise and assist in curriculum development in all areas and on classroom procedures and management

12. organise a system of storage and retrieval for catalogues and price lists to be available for staff reference

13. coordinate and advise on assemblies, including daily class and special assemblies

14. assume responsibility under Health and Safety at Work policy for any immediate action, ensuring the cleanliness and safety of the working conditions of the school, and to inform the Headteacher of any immediate response

15. represent the Headteacher at all meetings at which he or she is not present, including Governors' meetings in his or her unavoidable absence

16. coordinate any school trips, visits by outside speakers and so on, ensuring that the details of organisation are sufficient in terms of aptness, safety precautions and insurance cover

17. assist in all curriculum areas and possibly accept responsibility in one or more of them.

Oil in the cogs

Once you have negotiated and agreed your job specification, it is tempting to presume that you are completely clear about what is expected.

What did you do at school today?

Dealing with minor issues

One of the major factors in the issue of support is assisting with the smooth running of the establishment. The Deputy Headteacher is the one who carries the oil can and many other cans. People will not notice when all goes well but they certainly will if it goes wrong. Teachers and children rarely comment that the playground is 'dog free'. One dog appears – send for the Deputy. It is also a well-known fact that Deputies throughout the land spend time dealing with issues which relate to toilets – there is no advice forthcoming in this book. We don't want to get bogged down in such detail!

The fact that you as a Deputy assist so much with the smooth running of the school should not be devalued. Although it is not advocated that the Deputy Headteacher becomes immersed in mundane matters, dealing with difficulties which will otherwise hinder or disrupt the school is one of the major aspects of being **responsive**.

To summarise, the Deputy will have responsibilities which can be defined. They will also need to be responsive to colleagues, children and others.

School inspection/ review process

Not only will you need to be responsive to the needs of the aforementioned Headteacher, teachers, children and so on, you will, if you are to be effective, need to be responsive to the Inspectors. One school which received a glowing inspection report contained a section on the fact that the school and, in particular, the caretaker, was warm and friendly – in other words, he made them repeated cups of tea.

In order for the school to be seen in its best light, Inspectors should be treated as visitors and you should aim to give a favourable impression. One suggestion that you could take on board is to leave request forms in the Inspectors' room (see Schedule 5).

Information for Inspectors

Health and Safety

The fire and emergency procedures are _____

_____

Parking arrangements _____

Security arrangements _____

Use of portable electrical equipment _____

Dining arrangements

Special dietary needs

_____

_____

How to order/pay for lunch

_____

_____

Arrangements for tea/coffee

_____

_____

Late evening tea/coffee

_____

_____

Dining arrangements		
Date _____		
	am	**pm**
Names of Inspectors		
Any other requests:		

Please indicate other requirements.

Leave the pro forma for dining arrangements each day.
Make sure someone collects the pro forma at a set time each day.

Preparation for inspection or review

It is true that all schools prepare for an inspection. It is also true that when cosmetic improvements are made (new plants everywhere) just before the team arrives, it is obvious. Schools do receive plenty of advance warning of an inspection and it is important that you and your Headteacher plan carefully for the event.

You should consider planning strategies for:

✔ reviewing your last inspection report and action plan
✔ having your finger on the pulse with parents
✔ observing teaching
✔ monitoring standards
✔ supporting coordinators
✔ researching current trends
✔ working closely with your Headteacher and senior management team.

In each school the opportunities for preparation will vary. It is an excellent idea to prepare your own action plan (see Schedule 6).

Initial visit of team leader

This will occur about two months prior to the inspection. The team leader will wish to view the school and meet people. First impressions do count, so be prepared. Offer to timetable the day and have staff in the right place at the right time for meetings.

During inspection

During any inspection or review period you will face enormous demands. Everybody will need your support and want you to be responsive to their needs. If possible, clear any non-contact time you have such as dinner-time duty for the week. Be available to talk, listen, suggest, advise and, most of all, implement and reinforce confidence.

Post inspection

Virtually every school finds this a difficult time. Staff may feel it is an anti-climax and will be elated but drained of most of their energy. Everyone will be anxious to know how well he or she did. It is likely that you will be invited to the verbal feedback to your Headteacher from the team leader. At this meeting your Headteacher may only hear the negative comment – it is like watching yourself on video, only the bad parts leap out at you. Try to remain detached; offer to take notes. Emphasise the positive points that are always there. Help the Headteacher to feed information back to the staff as soon as possible.

Post inspection stress

This is not a mythical phenomenon, it is a real living experience for most staff (particularly the Headteacher). Arrange a small celebration, nothing too elaborate as everyone will be tired and may not appreciate a dinner dance!

Be aware that staff and children may need you more than ever in the weeks following an inspection.

At times like these you can, and probably will, feel more like a dogsbody than on any other occasion but you must remember that every positive finding and every success occurred because you assisted. It is like being an anonymous donor to charity. You will gain satisfaction from your unseen contribution.

Inspection preparation

Aspect	Suggestion	Your action
Previous inspection	Read and review previous report and action plan.	
Parents	Conduct an inspection-style questionnaire six months before inspection. Be out on the playground before school. Dismiss your class from the playground and be available at home time.	
Observing teaching	Timetable yourself and give feedback against agreed criteria. If release from class is not possible, visit classrooms after school and discuss lessons with staff.	
Monitoring standards	Check planning and record-keeping. On a rotational basis, see pupils' work.	
Coordinators	Suggest they keep a diary or simple log of curriculum development activities (useful for inspection interviews). Make planning available. Discuss children's work and any analysis of tests. Offer practice interviews.	
Current trends	Read local inspection reports. Access recent inspection reports from your nominated team (Internet is useful – check you can read PDF files). Study any recent legislation.	
Headteacher and senior managers	Offer to collate documentation. Offer to help the Headteacher form a statement. Have regular meetings with SMT.	

Chapter

3

From policy to practice

Your Headteacher negotiates a task with you such as:

'Draw up new guidelines for the English Curriculum.'

You spend three weeks supporting the curriculum leader and involving colleagues:

YOU HAVE A COMMUNICATION PROBLEM!

and you have wasted three weeks. This is, of course, a gross exaggeration but the scenario is not uncommon.

It is absolutely essential, when putting policy into practice, that you establish what the policy will mean in real terms. In order to define these real terms it is necessary to set OBJECTIVES. Most teachers have an aversion to the word 'objectives' since they spent so many hours preparing lesson plans while on teaching practice.

Setting objectives

Let us be clear:

✔ What are objectives?
✔ How can they help the Deputy to support the policies of the school?

An objective is:

A statement or criterion which defines how policy will look when implemented.

An objective must be:

✔ clear

✔ concise

✔ written down

✔ time boundaried

✔ measurable

✔ and, above all, achievable.

Using the last example, the Deputy Headteacher needed a much clearer statement of objective such as:

'We need curriculum guidelines for Literacy which complement/reflect the National Curriculum. I would like a summary of the contents agreed by the staff by ... (given date).'

If the Deputy felt that this would not be achievable, this would be the correct time to say so. If this is the Deputy's opinion then he or she needs to seek advice from the Headteacher or request a readjustment of the objective. All too often the objective is not agreed, the criteria are not communicated and the result is disappointment and dissatisfaction.

Once the policy has been defined in these terms it is likely to be up to you how it can be achieved successfully.

Planning strategy

A practical and concise method of planning is to use a diagrammatic model which illustrates the following:

1. the starting point

2. steps along the way

3. completion; in other words, practice.

This model can take many forms, for example:

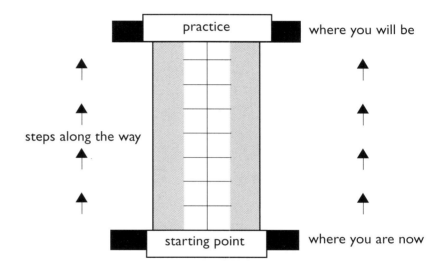

One important aspect of this method is that colleagues should be involved at the outset. It is the ideal opportunity for others to be included, voice their opinions and give of their expertise; this will encourage ownership of the process and the final policy.

Having established the overall objective, the first stage is to determine 'where you are now'. This exercise can take the form of a tick sheet, written ideas, group discussion and feedback and/or a summary produced by the curriculum leader for discussion and consensus.

The next stage is to define the steps along the way, who is to be responsible for each step and the completion date.

School policy

Here is an example which is likely to be given to any Deputy regardless of your school size.

Resolution

'Due to statements in the national press, the Governing Body expresses concern about bullying in schools and accordingly has formed a committee, chaired by the Deputy Headteacher, to produce a school policy document on this matter.'

The Governing Body has requested a policy statement and you are responsible for guiding the committee in its formulation.

Step 1. Define the objective clearly.

Step 2. Request a completion date.

Step 3. Request initial staff meeting time.

In this example let us suppose that the completion date is in 12 weeks time, beginning 4 September, and the committee has agreed to meet fortnightly when necessary.

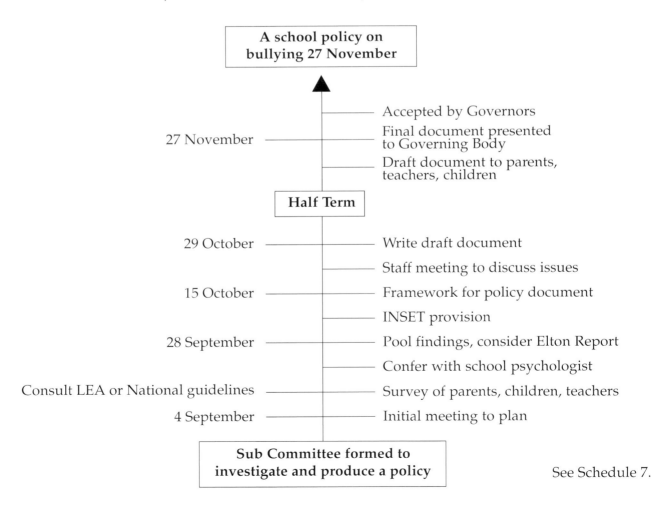

A school policy on bullying 27 November

27 November
- Accepted by Governors
- Final document presented to Governing Body
- Draft document to parents, teachers, children

Half Term

29 October — Write draft document

— Staff meeting to discuss issues

15 October — Framework for policy document

— INSET provision

28 September — Pool findings, consider Elton Report

— Confer with school psychologist

Consult LEA or National guidelines — Survey of parents, children, teachers

4 September — Initial meeting to plan

Sub Committee formed to investigate and produce a policy

See Schedule 7.

Action plan

Title . . . .

Problem solving

During the planning stage it is imperative that you consider hindrances that are likely to occur. Again, this is probably best illustrated using the same example.

A member of the committee, a Mr B. Beef, is slightly to the right of Genghis Khan and his idea of discipline is based on the philosophy of short sharp shock or bully the bullies. This will make you aware that a softly softly approach of counselling bullies is unlikely to meet his approval.

Result: You are clear on the direction; however, there is an obstacle. To try to ignore this obstacle until you are forced to confront it is to doom the strategy to failure.

There is only one way to deal with a similar situation!
You have choices (and, remember, consequences):

Dealing with an obstacle

Possible solutions:

✔ Ignore him or her.

✔ Bully HIM or HER.

✔ Try to accommodate his or her opinion.

✔ Bring about a shift in his or her position.

Bully HIM.

If you are aware of the problem you can adjust the strategy. In this instance, you could ask Mr Beef to be part of a group investigating the Elton Report. If this does not bring about a shift in his opinions, you must ensure that any working group from the committee has strong enough personalities and opinions to counter him.

Allies

When planning a strategy it is tempting to concentrate on perceived problems. It is more important to identify those who will assist in providing and maintaining momentum, in other words, your potential allies.

. . . someone who will 'combine, unite for a special objective'.

An ally is defined in the dictionary as someone who will: 'combine, unite for a special objective', for example, a useful ally to use with Mr Beef may be a specialist support teacher.

Where allies may be found:

✔ colleagues in school

✔ inset providers

✔ parents

✔ governors

✔ occasionally, a national document.

It may be helpful to list your potential allies and define the qualities and/or experience that will assist you.

IS ALL OF THIS NECESSARY?

Answer – No! – But!

When faced with planning policy it is tempting to think that the following is too much work:

✔ defining objectives
✔ planning a strategy
✔ using allies.

One theme that will be addressed in the next chapter is classroom practice. Time spent carefully researching, planning and preparing work for a classroom makes the job of the class teacher easier in the long run.

Sandpapering a door may be tedious but when you begin to paint it is much easier, the finished product is longer lasting and the rewards are greater.

Managing big and little people

Classroom skills

It is likely that one of the main reasons you were appointed was that you are an excellent classroom practitioner. You were trained for that role at college, you built on that through experience and were assisted and developed by more experienced colleagues. Your expertise and experience lie in this field.

Management skills

Is it not often said that the best teachers do not always make the best managers? It is unlikely that you have been trained, developed or have much experience of management as a Deputy Headteacher. You have been appointed to a job for which there is no specific qualification and your training has probably been limited. LEAs and the central government agencies are advocating the identification of potential senior managers at an earlier stage and it is to be hoped that these moves are realised. The question is, can all that accumulated experience and knowledge of classroom practice be transferred to your present role as a senior manager?

Management potential

Every teacher who teaches a group of up to 35 individuals and organises a classroom has extensive managerial experience and skills. Teachers are renowned for being excellent organisers of materials and children. In the world at large, teachers invariably serve on committees, society groups, and so on and you have only to glance at *The Times Educational Supplement* to see the number of companies anxious to recruit teachers and utilise their skills. There is a growing tendency to see one aspect of the teacher's job as **manager** of the classroom/curriculum. There are now courses and books entitled 'The Teacher as Manager'.

Teachers manage little people and yet are often uncomfortable managing big people. Give a teacher 200 children to manage in a playground – no problem. Ask a teacher to manage a group of colleagues and they feel uneasy.

> The skills and knowledge gleaned from the classroom can and do transfer directly to senior management positions and that is why an excellent classroom practitioner has the potential to become a most effective manager.

Dealing with behaviour problems

Whenever faced with a difficult or uncomfortable situation, it is a worthwhile exercise to try to transfer the problem and see it in terms of classroom dynamics. Take as an example a teacher who lacks confidence.

In the classroom: if a child lacks confidence the teacher would set them up to succeed, praise and encourage them and congratulate their success. This would then be built on to take the child further.

The same can apply to an adult.

Consider these two lists of types of behaviour. All teachers have experienced them in the classroom and, as Deputy, you may well experience them in the staffroom.

A	B
Little experience	Hogs limelight
Low motivation	Poor timekeeping
Low competence	Poor attendance
Lack of confidence	Over confident
Not fulfilling potential	Aggressive
Unwilling to take responsibility	Bad-mannered
Not popular	Disorganised

In the classroom you would deal naturally with these behaviours; if a strategy you chose did not work you would try another. Normally, you would view a difficult child as a challenge. It is considered unthinkable for a teacher to give up on a child. However, when these behaviours occur in adults they appear far more threatening and there is a tendency to avoid addressing them.

Children always prefer a teacher who makes it quite clear what is acceptable, fair, and with whom they know where they stand.

Whenever a child is exhibiting one such behaviour, teachers generally use a wide range of strategies. However, whichever strategies are chosen they usually fall into one of two categories – positive or negative comments.

Supporting colleagues

Look again at the two lists on page 27.

List A behaviours are best changed by encouragement and by setting the person up to succeed.

List B behaviours would be best dealt with by pointing out that these are unacceptable and detract from the individual, as well as showing them how to put things right.

Both of these strategies are clear indicators of the main role of the Deputy – to support.

This support is best given by using praise or by honest discussion coupled with positive, constructive suggestions.

Positive comments

In order to praise a person they must be able to succeed. It will sound hollow if the praise is not genuine. The skill of praising is setting people up to succeed and then IDENTIFYING their successes.

Praise is far more effective if you include in your conversation how it makes you FEEL.

For example, 'I always enjoy showing someone your classroom. Your display work is very good'.

Negative comments

The key to reprimanding a behaviour is that it is the behaviour you are criticising, not the person. (Consider how you tell a child off.)

After a reprimand, it is essential that the person is left thinking about their behaviour, not yours, and knows how to put it right.

"If I have to mention timekeeping to you again ..."

For example, 'I hate having to do this but I have to mention timekeeping to you again. How can I help you to sort out this problem?'

Credibility

You will remember the feelings of fear that surrounded your first teaching practice. Fear that the children would not behave, that you would run out of material and that the children would know you were 'only' a student. As your confidence grew, these feelings diminished.

The same type of feelings will be aroused when you become a Deputy. You may worry that your colleagues will not respect you, you will not live up to the expectations and perhaps you are concerned that you lack experience in certain areas.

As a student and as a Deputy these feelings arise because you may doubt your own credibility. What is worse is that your colleagues may also harbour misgivings. The underlying inference of the question that you may perceive is:

> *'I am more experienced – who do you think you are?'*

Many Deputies have been asked the question:

> *'Have you ever taught this age group?'*

You cannot be an expert and all-knowing in every field and it is inadvisable to pretend that you are. It is worth considering your weaknesses or lack of experience and deciding whether it is necessary to address particular aspects. If you have little or no experience of nursery education but that department in your school is obviously run extremely well, it would be unnecessary to devote time and effort to researching this field. If there appears to be a problem, you should take steps to gain the necessary knowledge and understanding to be able to support the department's development.

A peculiar British cultural trait is that we do not feel at ease identifying our strengths. It is, however, essential to view weaknesses and strengths together. Recognising your strengths and weaknesses is a strength in itself. Schedule 8 provides a useful self-analysis format.

Strengths and weaknesses

I am good at

I have experience of

I am not good at

Weaknesses I need
to address

Methods to bring
about desired
changes

Chapter

5

Do you recall the golden age of teaching when all the children had the same ability, they were all well-behaved, no one was ever late, the work needed no corrections and teachers were home by 4.30pm, pouring themselves sweet sherry before listening to the radio?

The golden age of teaching.

If you don't remember this you are obviously living in the highly pressured, fast-moving, real world – but remember, until the government declares otherwise ...

THERE ARE 24 HOURS IN A DAY!

We have all met teachers who work extremely hard and yet are relatively ineffective, and others who have the knack of not being under pressure.

Every Deputy Headteacher should watch a video of Bobby Charlton playing football. He was rarely tackled, never hurried and always had space. The reason was he 'played smart'. The key to managing time is to work smarter, not harder. There is no secret to time management; however, there are ways of working smarter to use time more effectively.

Saying No!

This is the most obvious and yet the most difficult way. Often you will take on a task yourself for the following reasons:

- ✔ It will be done well.
- ✔ It will be done on time.
- ✔ The person who should do it isn't on the ball.
- ✔ You won't have to rely on others.

If you find yourself in this position, step back and reflect on the job of the Deputy Headteacher. Being a Deputy Headteacher is not always about producing a Mathematics or Science policy, it is more usually about supporting others to produce that policy. The finished product may not be up to your 'incredibly high standard' but, when complete, it can be a milestone and a step for further progression for that member of staff.

When it actually comes to saying 'no' there are all kinds of emotions that will arise. Your natural reaction is to want to please and become all things to all people. It is impossible to become all things to all people and to attempt it will lead to dissatisfaction and resentment.

It is impossible to become all things to all people.

Your job is NOT to do everything yourself but to enable and support others to do their jobs effectively. The rule of thumb is – if you are doing a task for which someone else is responsible you are not 'working smart'.

If you really do need to say 'no', a sharp retort and stamp of the foot will cause conflict. Far better to put your 'no' in context or offer a choice, for example, 'I can organise the sports day if you want me to, however, I will not be able to do it as well as you could.'

Dividing work into sizeable chunks

Whenever asked to take on a task, always plan it out methodically and practically before you agree to a timescale for completion. That is, break the task into sizeable chunks. For example: two months to formulate a policy for the PTA is adequate but not if it straddles Christmas. Work out a time plan and allow for any planned or major school events. Only commit yourself to that which is, in your opinion, achievable.

Using objectives in time management

Sizeable chunks are objectives or stages along the way. The purpose of objectives in time management is that they are indicators of progress, in other words 'the job isn't complete but I'm still on course'. It is tempting to lose sight of progress and become impatient. Progress is success and you, of all people, need to identify the markers along the way.

Use of diary

It is essential that Deputy Headteachers develop good diary practice. There are many recommended ways to organise your diary.

For example, divide into am and pm or list and prioritise.

One simple yet effective method is to use a week-to-week diary and divide the page into three columns: Deputy Headteacher's Jobs (You), School and Pupils, and Headteacher.

It is also a good idea to use the Saturday and Sunday spaces to note more general or ongoing matters which need your attention or consideration.

Weekly planning

Half an hour at home over the weekend considering tasks and ordering your thoughts is worth at least two hours during the week, when you are likely to have constant interruptions. Tasks for the coming week can be considered as goals and if you miss them you can shoot again the next week.

Non-contact time should be allocated to developing ongoing projects. It is tempting to use this time to deal with matters which concern the smooth running of the school, your department or class. To do this can lead to crisis management because all too often non-contact time for a Deputy Headteacher can be disrupted. View this valuable time as committed, not as a chance to catch up.

This is **as** important for both class teaching Deputies, who are tempted to use the time to catch up with assessment or display, and non-class teaching Deputies, who use the time to sort out rotas and social problems. These kinds of tasks have a bad habit of expanding to fill the time available. The Deputy Headteacher can so easily feel the martyr, the pig in the middle, the first mate, the general dogsbody and so on. The message is loud and clear. The key to time management is to control your own time.

Chapter

6

Financial management

The 1988 Education Act heralded the arrival of the Local Management of Schools, that is, most schools, depending upon size, would have control of their own budgets. Things have moved on a long way since then. Initial fears and worries of Headteachers and Governors have been allayed as schools have realised they have much more control. It should be borne in mind that financial management is not the quagmire or straitjacket it was once made out to be. A basic understanding of terms and principles is required so that one has a working knowledge and this in itself will dispel the aura of mystery which surrounds it.

Previous chapters outlined the importance of the Deputy's role in the running of the school. All Deputies, no matter what size of school they work in, will need a working knowledge of devolvement of finance to their own school. The involvement of the Deputy will depend upon the size of the school and the expectations of the Head and Governors.

". . . so the school ends up with an amount of money to use."

Local management of schools

In 1998 the government stated its intention of developing what was 'Local Management of Schools' (LMS) with the aims of:

1. Simplifying delegation to schools.
2. Increasing the delegation to schools.

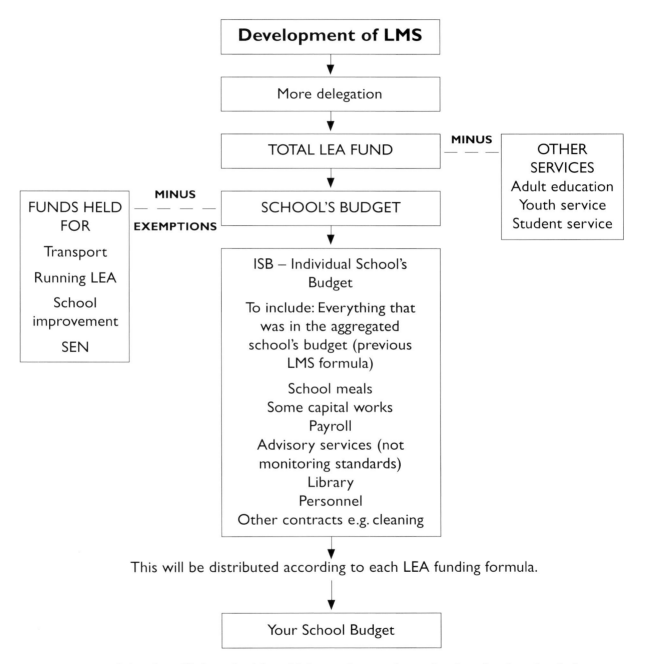

This will be distributed according to each LEA funding formula.

Schools will then decide which services and at what level to buy back from the LEA, and either choose to undertake them themselves or enter into private contracts.

WARNING – You can bet your next target-related pay rise that this will impact on the role of the Deputy!

How does this affect the school?

The Governing Body is responsible for setting this budget, the Headteacher is responsible for administering it. As part of the management team, it is essential that the Deputy spends some time going through the budget with the Head at the beginning of and during the financial year. This will give the Deputy an overall view of the health of the budget and also an insight into the priorities outlined. It may be apparent from the first glance at the budget that there is little room for manoeuvre as the majority of the funding is tied up in staffing costs (particularly teaching staff).

Specific responsibilities

There will also be money allocated to budget headings such as equipment capitation, fuel costs, ground maintenance, cleaning and even for trade waste (emptying the bins). The amount of money committed to staffing highlights the increasingly important role of the Deputy in enabling the teachers of the school to perform well. It is easy to lose sight of the big picture and become too cash-orientated. You may well raise £200 by holding a Saturday car boot sale, but consider the extra work and stress for members of staff and particularly you! Is this cost effective?

On a functional level, the Deputy may be required to perform certain duties or take on particular responsibilities in the administration of the budget. These will vary. The Deputy may be asked to become an expert on the school computer system or be asked to switch off the lights. The scope of responsibility could be awe inspiring (don't be surprised if toilets and/or water supply figure highly).

Don't be surprised if toilets and/or water supply figure highly.

Supply costs

A Deputy will need to have a working knowledge of the budget and its administration. Of particular importance are supply costs (see Chapter 9 on Acting Headship). The Deputy should know the supply budget for the year and details of any staff absence, agency contracts and insurance schemes. This will enable the Deputy to decide whether supply cover can be brought in if there is an emergency.

Highly recommended

Your Governing Body will have established a committee for finance. It is recommended that the Deputy should attend meetings of this committee, either as an adviser/observer or in order to gain an appreciation of the budget and to be aware of mid-year financial pressures or fluctuations.

Setting the budget

In all budgetary considerations, managers are faced with a choice/consequence situation (as described in Chapter 2).

In the event of you having to set the budget due to the absence of your Headteacher, it is essential that you have by then gained as much experience as possible. In order to prepare yourself for such an eventuality, refer to Chapter 9 on Acting Headship (do not wait until your Headteacher breaks a leg). Ensure you are involved.

Ideally, the flexibility of a system where schools control their own budgets should allow governors and senior managers to be responsive to local needs. However, it can become very easy, unless you are careful, to see pound signs in place of children.

"Money is a terrible master but an excellent servant." *PT Barnum (1810–1891)*

The budget must serve the needs of the school and this is best reflected in a well-considered school development plan.

Chapter

7

The Home School comunity

Managing the Home School community

It is highly likely that, as Deputy Headteacher, you will assume some degree of responsibility for Home School partnerships, liaison and involvement. This is an area where many newly appointed Deputies see a chance to make their mark. However, managing the Home School community needs careful development.

Before making an attempt to develop this involvement, it is necessary that the Deputy Headteacher is clear about the degree and type of involvement appropriate to their school. There are many factors that will affect this association:

✔ Socio-economic background of the school.
✔ Past history of involvement.
✔ Attitudes of staff.

There are various models which illustrate the most appropriate way forward, depending on the above factors:

Model A
This is where parents come in to the school and assist with tasks and/or fundraising. Their work is supplementary and solely in the form of an official PTA or Friends' Association.

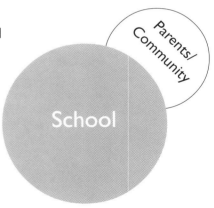

Model B
In this model parents are an integral part of the school and are actively involved, under the guidance of teachers, in the learning process and other areas of school life.

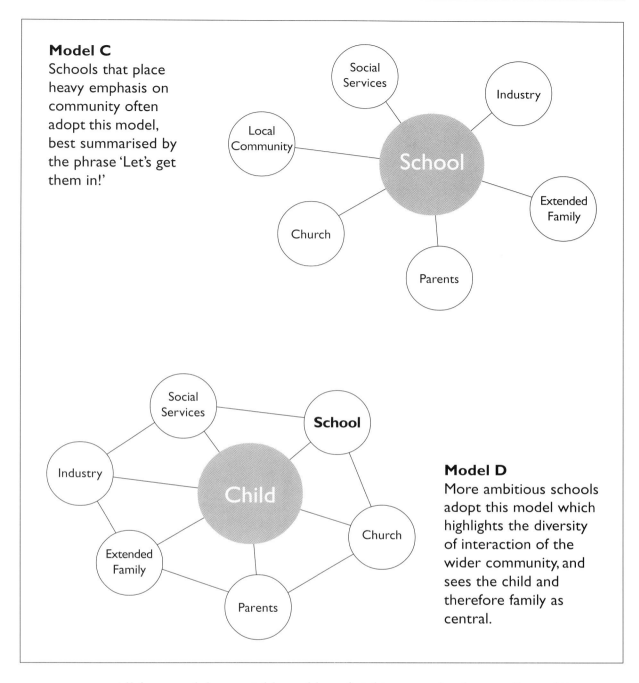

Model C
Schools that place heavy emphasis on community often adopt this model, best summarised by the phrase 'Let's get them in!'

Model D
More ambitious schools adopt this model which highlights the diversity of interaction of the wider community, and sees the child and therefore family as central.

All four models are viable and beneficial to any school, regardless of its circumstances.

Model D affords the greatest possibilities and scope for promoting involvement and creating a true home/school/community partnership. Schools have a great deal to offer the wider community and in doing so can enrich the learning process for their pupils. This model is wide enough in its scope to apply to any school, even one which has no history of Home School partnership and may have teachers who are reticent about having parents in their classrooms.

The central theme is that the Deputy be explicit and communicate the envisaged model to everyone concerned.

Creating a partnership

Teachers and others may need convincing as to the value of involvement with the wider community. To try to coerce teachers, parents and neighbours into becoming involved in a partnership can result in resentment and barriers being created.

The ideal approach is to seek out allies amongst the staff and parents. Build that partnership through those willing and interested – from this you can begin to establish a way forward.

The best way of planning this way forward is to seek advice, assistance from practitioners and, as a group, to research the possibilities.

It is essential that, given the role of coordinating community involvement, you make sure that the model you consider the most appropriate is shared by others, particularly your Headteacher and Governing Body.

Involvement with the wider community.

Chapter

8

Crisis management

Many handbooks make an attempt to prepare you for all eventualities. That is where *The Deputy Headteacher's Handbook* is different.

Crisis management is unlikely to have appeared in the advert for your Deputy Headship. It is, however, part and parcel of your role. Unexpected situations are often a feature of school life and you cannot be ready for every eventuality, but you can prepare to be flexible and able to respond.

Every teacher approaches the position of Deputy Headship with preconceived ideas and one or more role models. These ideas and models often result in an identity crisis which occurs two or three months into the job (and may re-occur). It is usually manifested by thoughts such as:

Rest assured, these feelings are shared, if not verbalised, by Deputy Headteachers throughout the land.

Communicating effectively

You must ensure that time is set aside for meetings with your Headteacher to compare diaries.

These meetings should be at the beginning of each half-term for forward planning and on a weekly basis for day-to-day occurrences. Regular set meetings of this nature fulfil a dual role.

1. They clarify who needs to be informed regarding different issues.
2. They ensure that you, the Deputy, are aware of the full spectrum of school events.

These outcomes are vital for all Deputies, particularly for the majority who have full-time class responsibility.

Disseminating information

The information then needs to be disseminated and you must decide on the most effective method of communication. The methods are many and will vary from school to school. The size of your establishment will often determine the most appropriate ways.

Whether yours is a large or small school, by far the best method is via short briefing meetings involving Headteacher/Deputy and all teachers. Ideally, these should occur each morning before school starts. The purpose of these meetings is to inform colleagues of forthcoming events, visitors, the availability of resources or to give general notices. These meetings should be formal and brief.

The value of briefing meetings

Briefing meetings are an effective strategy, they:

✔ eliminate the need to use valuable main staff meeting time for routine information

✔ alleviate the necessity for notes travelling around school (which is regularly a common cause of disturbance and complaint). Some schools have a formal system of a staff notice book which requires teachers' signatures or initials

✔ cut down the number of entries in the staff notice book but do not necessarily remove the need for it. For example, it is good practice to have teachers' signatures alongside notices dealing with aspects of safety or supervision.

Taking responsibility for communication in a school is a vital aspect of the Deputy's role and can circumvent many potential crises.

Effective communication is time consuming to establish and the benefits will only be noticed by other members of staff when it goes wrong. This illustrates the main contribution of the Deputy Headteacher; the effects are widespread but not tangible.

Whose diary was correct . . . ?

Question – Whose diary was correct, the police band's or yours?

Problem – Does school miss the opportunity of enjoying the band or do you upset Ms Vulcan who has just set up the PE apparatus with the reception class?

Result – Faced with similar situations you, and perhaps others, will question your performance and even your sanity. However, don't despair, there are a number of strategies and tools that can help you avoid being caught on the hoof.

Most difficulties which land in the Deputy Headteacher's lap will be the result of poor communication. The solution is that you take responsibility for ensuring effective communication. For example – if you know from experience that certain teachers do not go into the staffroom at break time and that others never read the notice board, then it is pointless putting up a notice to rearrange assembly time. The tendency is to put the notice up anyway and then blame colleagues. Taking responsibility for communication means ensuring that the information gets through.

Making your mark

As a Deputy you will feel the need to justify your position, to earn respect – in other words, to make your mark.

You know that you were appointed for your unique qualities, ideas and contribution. In order to 'make your mark', recognise your strengths, consider your short-term objectives and channel your energies into an aspect of school life that is:

✔ not stepping on people's toes
✔ high profile within the school
✔ achievable by you with easily recognisable results.

Your first priority if you have full-time class responsibility should be to make your room, your practice and your children an example to others.

Ways to make an impression

Plan a curriculum event for your class:

✔ A display in a central area of the school.

✔ A mini enterprise.

✔ Arranging different visits outside school or visitors to school.

✔ Involve parents and community.

✔ Organise a sports/arts/music festival.

✔ A coach trip after school for families.

✔ A unique fund-raising event.

Obtain resources from:

✔ Local high schools/industry.

✔ Teacher advisory support services.

Attract publicity.

An excellent idea is to attract good publicity for the school using local newspapers/radio. It is helpful to plan an activity/event which you know will be successful; for example, an idea from your previous school. (But don't say 'In my last school ...'.)

Taking assemblies

As a Deputy Headteacher, you will be expected to conduct school assemblies. This is often a source of anxiety; the sad fact is that there are no courses on conducting assemblies and few schools see it as requiring INSET.

As a newly qualified teacher you will have marvelled at the ease with which an experienced teacher could organise their classroom. If you were fortunate they would have passed on some useful tips to you.

The same is true of taking assembly. Schools will differ in the way they view what is acceptable concerning content and conduct and there are tried and tested guidelines to assist you.

Surviving assemblies

Watch and learn from an expert.

Before Assembly:

DO	DON'T
1 plan the format	1 Sh! Sh! Sh! Sh! Sh! Sh! You will remind the children of Thomas the Tank Engine
2 read through your material first	
3 tell a story if you can	2 walk around too much
4 work out the order for classes leaving assembly so that it can be effected quickly and smoothly	3 stand behind a lectern or table
	4 stand too close to or 'on top of' particularly young children
5 be in the hall first – if necessary with your class	5 raise your voice unless it is for effect
6 use a lectern or table as a prop if necessary.	6 read a story too quickly.

During Assembly

DO

1 demand everyone's attention at the start

2 ask the children to stop being noisy. When you have their attention, start again. If necessary stand them all up and then ask them to sit quietly

3 stand comfortably and scan the room

4 make eye contact with as many children as possible

5 personally address a child you consider is misbehaving or is bad-mannered.

DON'T

1 carry on if you are losing the children's attention – ask a question which you are sure can be answered

2 always expect a correct answer from the Reception children

3 ask rhetorical questions (unless your assembly is pantomime style)

4 ask for volunteers – just choose (sensitively)

5 encourage interruptions during a story.

The content

Introduce with a personal experience.

Make the material relevant.

Use children and props where possible (choose carefully and sensitively).

Insist on raised hands in answer to a question.

Limit the number of wrong answers (the children become bored).

At the end of the Assembly

DO

1 ensure that teachers are with or are ready to receive their classes

2 insist that children leave the hall in the manner which is appropriate in your school.

NEVER

1 trip over the naughty child you have placed behind you

2 use names or words which will cause sniggers, for example 'Dick'.

Assembly time provides an excellent opportunity for promoting a culture of praise and validating school values.

A Deputy is often called upon to produce an assembly at very short notice. Always have at least two assemblies, appropriate for any age group, to hand.

Lesson at short notice

There will be occasions when every Deputy is faced with:

- ✔ taking a class (or more than one) at short notice
- ✔ being called away from your own class
- ✔ having your attention diverted from your planned programme.

Adequate preparation for these eventualities will reduce stress and counteract negative effects upon the children. A class teaching Deputy needs to have available a package with a plan which includes self-supporting activities and the necessary resources.

A Deputy without class responsibility would be wise to have available sufficient packages to suit all age groups within the school. (See Schedule 9.)

Having your attention diverted from your planned programme ...

A lesson at a moment's notice

Substituting in a class

It is advisable to have lessons planned to cover all age ranges (not necessarily your own group).

When choosing subject content look to your own curriculum strengths.

Age range	**Duration**
Resources: **Teacher** **Children**	
Ground rules	
Learning outcomes	
Introduction	
Activities/development	
Extension activities	

1. Make as much of the content as self-supporting as possible; this will give you time to plan a more extended programme.

2. Make full use of any ancillary assistance available, particularly with Nursery or infants. Have all resources prepared, including a supply of pencils, paper and so on. 'Have chalk, will travel.'

Chapter

9

Acting Headship

No matter how robust and healthy your Headteacher, you need to prepare for Acting Headship. Every Deputy Head will be required to cover for short periods when the Headteacher is attending meetings and so on, and may, due to circumstances, be in this position for a longer period of time.

The first occasion on which you are left in charge can be quite daunting. Given that you have probably looked forward to this very responsibility, it will have come as a surprise that you feel apprehensive. This is a natural feeling and occurs when anyone faces a new challenge.

When a Deputy is Acting Head there is often confusion as to whether they are really in charge or whether they are a 'caretaker Head'. The fact is, in many respects you are 'minding the shop', but it is vital that you recognise that you are answerable and accountable for things that occur in the school. This is the overriding principle, however, your approach will alter according to the duration of your Acting Headship.

It would be wonderful if every absence of your Headteacher could be predicted. It cannot and therefore you must take measures to ensure that you are prepared for this eventuality.

The most common cause of panic amongst Deputies in this position is PAPERWORK!

Paperwork

The forms! It is a truism that at any time of the year at least fifty per cent of schools have not completed fifty per cent of the administrative documents or sent them in on time. So do not worry too much. If a form that you have:

- ✔ made a mess of
- ✔ never filled in
- ✔ never heard of

is important then a clerical assistant from the local or national administration will contact you (you will not be alone).

Certain forms are more important than life itself but these relate exclusively to wages and salaries. People will quickly point out any mistakes you make in this area. Excuses such as 'I do not know much about these forms' will fall on deaf ears.

To prepare for Acting Headship it is wise to ask your Headteacher to help you to complete Schedule 10 in order to identify weekly, monthly and annual returns.

Returns form

Weekly

Name/Form number	Completed by	Signed by	Sent to

Monthly

Name/Form number	Completed by	Signed by	Sent to

Termly/Annually

Name/Form number	Completed by	Signed by	Sent to

It is wise to keep and file a copy of any return you complete. The school secretary should be aware of the location of each form. If the secretary is part-time, make sure you know where things are filed.

Primary Professional Development – The Deputy Headteacher's Handbook   © Folens (copiable page)

The main issues

Although paperwork is often the major cause of concern, the most important areas are in fact those that relate to the children in your care. It is recommended that you complete Schedule 11 to ensure that you are *aufait* with:

- ✔ addresses and emergency telephone numbers
- ✔ legal and access orders
- ✔ medical and health conditions
- ✔ travel arrangements.

This schedule also includes other aspects of internal organisation that you should be aware of. It is annoying when the burglar alarm sounds and nobody knows where the key is or how to switch it off.

Finally, your Headteacher will have extensive experience of the Local Authority and Support Services and is the best source to help you formulate a list of people who can be relied upon for sound advice or information, should you require it.

Often the best person from whom to seek advice is a Headteacher of a local school (Schedule 12). Your Headteacher will know who is approachable and will be willing to be of assistance. Do not be afraid to ask, as seeking advice is preferable to making serious mistakes, and remember – experts enjoy sharing their knowledge.

Short-term Acting Headship

'Now everyone is out of the way . . .'

For this purpose short term is defined as no more than one week. The very nature of the Headteacher's role will mean that they are required to attend meetings, conferences and so on. Therefore, this type of cover is becoming more frequent. The very last thing that the Headteacher wishes to return to is a drama or a crisis. As with babysitting, the Headteacher wants the school to be looked after well.

The systems already established within the school will be sufficient to deal with most situations and if you have carefully noted the advice in the previous section all should go well.

Acting Headship checklist

Children

1. Location of addresses and emergency telephone numbers. ☐
2. Medical conditions. ☐
3. Access and legal orders. ☐
4. Travel arrangements including coach/taxi phone numbers. ☐

Building

1. Caretaker's/Site Manager's home telephone numbers. ☐
2. Caretaker's hours. ☐
3. Location keys for:

    Fire alarm ☐

    Burglar alarm ☐

    Boiler house ☐

    Other locked areas. ☐

Emergency procedures

1. Fire regulations. ☐
2. Accident procedures. ☐
3. Hospital telephone number. ☐
4. Local authority telephone number. ☐
5. Dog warden telephone number. ☐
6. Social services telephone number. ☐
7. Local police station telephone number. ☐

Complete this checklist and ensure that you have all the necessary information in an accessible place.

Advice

Who to go to	Contact name	Phone number
1. Headteacher of neighbouring school		
2. Local Authority		
Health and Safety		
Teacher/Staffing Supply		
School Adviser/Inspector		
Building Department		
Ancillary staffing		
Others		
3. Chair of Governors		
4. Police Liaison Officer		
5. Local taxi (contract)		
6. Teachers' Centre		
7. Swimming pool		
8. Local schools		
9. Student/College Supervisors		
10. Meals Supervisor		
11. Child Guidance/Psychologist		
12. Clinic/Health Centre		
13. Union/Association Secretary		

Complete this checklist and ensure that you have all the necessary information.

Dealing with emergencies

Despite all precautions, emergencies can and do happen. These can take a variety of forms:

i) Accident involving children

The watchword must be 'take no chances'. If a child has an accident which appears more serious than normal, the first step is to decide whether or not an ambulance is necessary. Then contact the parents or guardian. If the child is sent to hospital and the parent cannot be contacted, assign a senior member of staff to accompany the child. Meanwhile, a letter should be left at the family home asking the parents to contact you at school as soon as possible. (Be sensitive with regard to the contents of the letter.) At the end of school, if the parents have still not contacted you, leave a further letter at the home asking them to contact you at the hospital. Make sure that the letter is brief and reassuring. You will then need to relieve the member of staff at the hospital. The next day you will need to complete the necessary accident forms and procedures.

ii) Child leaves the school premises

Ensure the child has left and is not asleep in the home corner, or anywhere else. Make a thorough initial search of the school and immediate area. Then contact the parents by phone. If parents cannot be contacted (as with the accident case) adopt a similar procedure for letters to the family home. If all else fails and the child cannot be found and there has been no contact with parents, refer the matter to the local police.

iii) Children not collected after school

Try to telephone parents or emergency contact numbers. If unsuccessful, take the child to their home. If no one is in and you have checked with the neighbours, again leave a letter for the parents, return with the child to school and wait for a reasonable time. In the unlikely event of no contact from the parents, notify Social Services.

All other matters concerning children should be dealt with by you according to the practices of the school.

Routine enquiries from parents

Most enquiries made by parents and referred to you should be dealt with as a matter of course; if there is a query which you cannot answer, inform the parent that you will make enquiries and will contact them the following day.

Long-term Acting Headship

Given that resignations may be left until the minimum required for statutory notice, it is not unusual for the Deputy to be Acting Headteacher for anything up to six months. The same principles that have already been outlined will apply. The major difference is that you cannot refer issues to the Headteacher and therefore the 'buck stops with you'. An irate parent is unlikely to agree to wait six months for the new appointee to arrive.

It is unwise as Acting Headteacher to instigate major policy or procedural changes unless they concern Health and Safety. It is a fact and often surprises Deputies in this position that their colleagues will rally round and offer support. Rely on your senior teachers and the school administrator, they will normally have a wealth of practical experience and will appreciate being asked for their opinion or advice. There is also unlimited experience and knowledge outside your school and in your Local Authority. If you are really 'lucky', your long-term Acting Headship occurs during the months of February and budget setting time. In conjunction with advice from the Local Authority and working closely with the governing body's sub-committee, you will need to set the budget for the following year.

Setting a budget

It is illegal to set a deficit budget. There are many principles which can be applied to budget planning, the most often used and certainly relevant for you as Acting Headteacher is a cost-based model:

---

1. Cost what you have already based on last year's prices. Make sure you get a copy of each year's outrun statement (i.e., final balance sheet).
2. Add for inflation/pay rises.
3. Can you afford the same?

Yes – leave things as they are. *No* – consider where savings can be made.

Above all, seek advice.

If you are in the fortunate position of growth, continue to follow the priorities identified in the school development plan.

Deputising for the Headteacher

It is not Acting Headship in its true definition but you may be required to deputise for your Headteacher.

At meetings, case conferences and so on

When attending such meetings, introduce yourself and give your Headteacher's apologies. Take notes and report to the Headteacher upon your return.

Chairing or attending Governors' committees

It is essential that before you attend such meetings you seek the views of the Headteacher and, where applicable, determine the most desired outcome. Remember that committees are delegated by the full Governing Body and will already have been given their remit. Make sure you are aware of the full scope of this remit and clarify the rules of this committee with the Clerk to the Governors. Finally, such committee meetings should be minuted.

Attending full Governors' meetings as Acting Headteacher

Each Governing Body is able to invite observers to attend meetings. You should request such an invitation before it becomes necessary for you to attend as Acting Headteacher.

Attending as appointed Acting Headteacher gives you the right to participate fully. The previous Minutes and each item on the agenda should be fully considered beforehand. It is advisable to inform your Chair of Governors before the meeting of any issues that you intend to raise.

Issues which may require clarification

Q *Is the Headteacher's signature required or can I sign?*

A You can usually sign all orders, authorisations, forms and so on. You may not be able to sign cheques. You need to check which signatory lists you are on.

Q *Can I use my judgement and bring in supply teachers?*

A Yes, bear in mind the policy of the school and its budget.

Q *Should a class teaching Deputy bring a supply in for their class in the event of the Headteacher's absence?*

A Not usually for short-term absence. Longer-term cover availability will depend upon the strength of the school budget and/or any existing insurance policies.

Q *Can the police interview a child on the school premises?*

A No, not without the consent of the parents.

Q *Can Social Services interview a child on the premises?*

A Yes, in exceptional circumstances, but it is advisable that you are present (check with a Local Authority Child Protection Officer).

Q *Can I exclude a child?*

A Yes, but it would be inadvisable. As a last resort, consult the Local Authority's Educational Welfare Department for advice.

Q *Can I close the school in case of emergency such as heating failure?*

A Not immediately. Your Local Authority will have issued guidelines and they should be contacted. Remember, schools have a legal obligation to give parents adequate notice depending upon the age of the children. You should also contact your Chair of Governors.

Finally, if you are Acting Headteacher because the post is vacant and you intend to apply, do not be tempted to make many changes to prove that you are the best candidate. The Governing Body will be impressed if you can continue to run the school smoothly during what is often an unsettling period.

'Can I close the school in case of emergency such as heating failure?'

Chapter

10

For those who decide that Headship is what you want, read on.

Often one of the essential criteria for Headships is a further qualification beyond initial training. The DfEE has introduced a National Professional Qualification for Headship initiative which will take at least one year to complete but may be extended over a longer time. It would be advisable to plan your period of study for this qualification in advance. Many Deputies have already embarked upon M.Ed or MA qualifications. These are highly relevant qualifications and, depending upon the stage you are at, you should take Local Authority advice on whether it is wise to complete the course or divert to the NPQH qualification. Often, depending upon your Local Authority criteria, successful completion of higher degree modules enhances your chances of support for the NPQH programme. (See Schedule 13.)

The Headteacher selection process

It must be appreciated that recent legislation has not only resulted in a delegation of financial responsibilities to Governing Bodies, but also includes the delegation of responsibilities for personnel issues. One major aspect is, of course, recruitment. Appointment procedures are complex and in most cases the Governing Body or, more appropriately its personnel committee, relies upon the Headteacher and the Local Authority representative for procedural advice.

If you decide to apply for a Headship it is essential that you appreciate the methods of selection for interview. It is impossible to be precise as practice will differ with each Local Authority and Governing Body. Governing Bodies are now responsible for the entire appointment procedure and there is a wide spectrum of approach for selection, many eliminate rather than choose candidates for interview. What follows will range from the traditional reasonable letter and half-hour interview (less common) to a more professional approach.

Appointment procedure

A common method is to:

✔ establish an appointments committee

✔ draw up job specification and person specification

✔ formulate an advertisement

✔ decide upon the details to be sent to those who make enquiries

✔ fix dates for shortlisting and interviews.

Planning for NPQH

All documentation and application forms are available from the Teacher's Training Agency – your Local Authority Staff Development Officer or your professional association or union will give you advice.

Funding is available to each Local Authority via the Standards Fund. Your application should be forwarded to the Local Authority Committee if you wish to apply for funding. This committee will assess your suitability for support.

Application can only be made three times each year on specific dates.

The fees for this qualification are expensive, so do apply in good time.

Read all the documentation attached to the application form carefully and leave plenty of time to complete the application. Some candidates are rejected at this stage because they do not address the criteria.

You are asked to give practical examples of your contribution towards the following:

✔ strategic direction and development of the school

✔ teaching and learning

✔ leading and managing staff

✔ efficient and effective development of staff and resources.

When your application has been accepted and recommended, it will be sent to a Regional Centre and an assessment of need will be completed. This will advise on the number of modules you need to complete the training.

The training consists of the compulsory module and further modules chosen by the candidate.

The training can be undertaken at a Regional Centre (often at weekends) or by Supported Open Learning with the Open University or your professional association.

The qualification will become mandatory in the near future.

Starting the process

A Requesting details

i.   Ensure your letter is of good quality; in other words, well written, courteous and precise. Remember, it might be filed.

ii. Enclose an A4 stamped addressed envelope.

B Research the school

i.   Drive around the catchment area.

ii. If a copy of the prospectus is not included in the details, ask for one at the local library.

iii. Discuss the school with your Headteacher/advisor.

Having acquired this information, you will be in a position to apply. It is remarkable the number of applicants who do not pay due regard to the details and information that they have received.

READ THEM CAREFULLY.

Your letter and curriculum vitae must address every item in the advertisement details and specifications. This cannot be over stressed, as failure to do so is the most common cause of not reaching the interview stage. All correspondence should be typed or completed in black ink as it will be photocopied.

Curriculum Vitae   Whether a CV is requested or not, it is wise to invest the time and effort necessary to produce one. There are professional companies which specialise in the compilation of CVs and the results can be impressive but expensive. There are also many model CVs in books and magazines. One simple yet effective model is included as Schedule 14. This is only a guide and it is recommended that you consider alternatives. It is always advisable to have your CV typed and well presented.

Application form   This should be typed unless your handwriting is particularly good. Read it carefully and complete it fully. Do not assume that because information is already in your CV it is not necessary.

Shortlisting

At shortlisting the governors, often with the assistance of the Local Authority representative, will have a list of:

A Essential criteria *(designed to eliminate unsuitable applicants)*

✔ A qualified teacher.

✔ Experience at senior management level.

✔ Attendance at relevant in-service training within the last three years.

✔ Experience of planning and organising major areas of the curriculum.

✔ Evidence of educational study beyond initial qualification.

B Desirable criteria

✔ Application addresses all key issues.

✔ Broad teaching experience across the age range.

✔ Knowledge of recent legislation and developments.

✔ A clear, well-considered and well-expressed philosophy of education.

N.B. These are not definitive lists, only examples. Criteria will be unique to each school. Applicants will be judged against these criteria and a shortlist drawn up.

Interviewing

The actual style of interview will again vary: it may be informal followed by a formal interview. You may be required to make a presentation or even teach a class.

At interview, regardless of the form it takes, there is likely to be a further list of criteria that will assist the selection panel in its decision-making process. These may include the following:

✔ appearance, body language, manner, confidence

✔ knowledge of the curriculum

✔ knowledge of management principles

✔ evidence of organisational skills

✔ a vision of the school's future.

'... body language, manner, confidence ...'

Curriculum Vitae

Application for the post of _____

at _____

1. Personal details

Name _____

Date of Birth _____

Address _____

_____

_____

Telephone No. (Home) _____ (Work) _____

Gender _____

Registered Disabled Yes/No   Number _____

DfEE/DES Number _____

N.I. Number _____

2. Education

Dates	School/College/University	Course Followed
Start with secondary education and follow chronologically. State full or part time.		

3. Qualifications

Dates	Qualifications	Institution
Start from 'O' level or equivalent up until most recent. Give exam grades and class of degree.		

(continued . . .

4. Employment history outside education

Dates	Position	Company

5. Employment history in education

Dates	Description	School/Education
	e.g. Responsibility points, Special Needs. (Do not include Teaching Practice.)	

6. Relevant in-service training

In this section only include Inset which is particularly relevant to the advertised post (REMEMBER THE DETAILS). Attach a sheet with further courses if necessary.

7. Present position

Description of major duties and responsibilities in list form, including any relevant involvement outside place of employment, e.g. Working Parties, Deputy Headteachers' Forum etc.

8. Interests

Be brief and interesting (everyone reads books).

9. Referees

Name		
Position		
Address		
Telephone		
Fax		

Do's and don'ts of applications

Do not

✔ be woolly or vague

✔ say

   – I think …

   – I am going to …

   – We are going to start a …

   – I was asked to be … (say I was offered and
     I was pleased to accept)

✔ make spelling or punctuation mistakes

✔ use a mass-produced letter and insert names.

Do

   ✔ give opinions

   ✔ state that you are eager for
     more responsibility

   ✔ stress that you have ideas that
     you wish to put into practice

   ✔ keep a copy of your letter, CV
     and application form

   ✔ explain irregularities such as
     career breaks.

Avoid

✔ story telling

✔ giving the impression that you are
  dissatisfied or disagree with your
  present manager

✔ dates, unless they illustrate a
  point

✔ sentences repeatedly beginning
  with I …

✔ use of jargon.

Your letter needs to be
concise; four sides of A4 would
be an absolute maximum and
two to three sides are
preferable. The selection panel
does not wish to read in detail
about your exploits at college
or first years of teaching.

Letter of application

It is essential that your letter of application addresses all the issues outlined in the job specification. The best advice when composing your letter is to approach the exercise as if you are already a Headteacher but are just waiting for the right school.

Do not take the standpoint that you are Super Deputy and therefore deserve the job. Although the selection panel does wish to know what you have achieved they will be more interested in what you have to offer their school.

Advice from colleagues

In order to place your application in perspective, your letter should contain an outline of your philosophy and approach to the Headship of this particular school. Rather than suggesting a standard format for a letter of application, the best advice is to seek advice from colleagues who have a successful track record. Your own Headteacher, other Headteachers and advisers have all been successful in applying for senior posts; pick their brains, ask them to read over your letter and make suggestions.

. . . ask them to read over your letter and make suggestions.